D1621927

Making Sense of the 2016 Elections

Sara Miller McCune founded SAGE Publishing in 1965 to support the dissemination of usable knowledge and educate a global community. SAGE publishes more than 1000 journals and over 800 new books each year, spanning a wide range of subject areas. Our growing selection of library products includes archives, data, case studies and video. SAGE remains majority owned by our founder and after her lifetime will become owned by a charitable trust that secures the company's continued independence.

Los Angeles | London | New Delhi | Singapore | Washington DC | Melbourne

Making Sense of the 2016 Elections

A CQ Press Guide

Brian Schaffner
University of Massachusetts Amherst

John A. Clark
Western Michigan University

SAGE | CQPRESS

FOR INFORMATION:

CQ Press
An Imprint of SAGE Publications, Inc.
2455 Teller Road
Thousand Oaks, California 91320
E-mail: order@sagepub.com

SAGE Publications Ltd.
1 Oliver's Yard
55 City Road
London EC1Y 1SP
United Kingdom

SAGE Publications India Pvt. Ltd.
B 1/I 1 Mohan Cooperative Industrial Area
Mathura Road, New Delhi 110 044
India

SAGE Publications Asia-Pacific Pte. Ltd.
3 Church Street
#10-04 Samsung Hub
Singapore 049483

Acquisitions Editor: Matthew Byrnie
Editorial Assistant: Zachary Hoskins
Production Editor: David C. Felts
Typesetter: C&M Digitals (P) Ltd.
Proofreader: Ellen Howard
Cover Designer: Anupama Krishnan
Marketing Manager: Amy Whitaker

Copyright © 2018 by CQ Press, an imprint of SAGE Publications, Inc. CQ Press is a registered trademark of Congressional Quarterly Inc.

All rights reserved. No part of this book may be reproduced or utilized in any form or by any means, electronic or mechanical, including photocopying, recording, or by any information storage and retrieval system, without permission in writing from the publisher.

Printed in the United States of America

ISBN 978-1-5063-8418-4

This book is printed on acid-free paper.

MIX
Paper from responsible sources
FSC® C012947

17 18 19 20 21 10 9 8 7 6 5 4 3 2 1

Contents

John Moore/Getty Images

Donald Trump's electoral college victory took many by surprise, as demonstrated by these shocked—and, in the case of the *Daily News*, horrified—cover pages from three New York City newspapers the morning after the general election.

Introduction

The 2016 election will undoubtedly leave a lasting impression on many Americans. A businessman and reality show star with no political experience whatsoever won the presidency despite losing to his opponent—the first ever female major party nominee for president—by over 2.8 million votes nationally. But it was also an election that will leave a lasting impression on political science. The success of Donald Trump's candidacy challenged many political science theories about the nature of American campaigns, while it simultaneously helped to highlight other important concepts that have long been well understood. In this volume, we revisit this historic election from the perspective of political science to provide important context about the 2016 election itself, and to consider how this election can inform our broader understanding of American politics.

The Electoral Landscape in 2016

Political scientists who study elections in the United States generally focus on a wide array of factors that might influence the outcome. These factors range from the general state of the economy in the months leading up to the election to where the candidates campaigned in the final weeks of the campaign. There are debates among scholars concerning the relative importance of each of these factors.[1] Indeed, many believe that the campaign is of minimal importance and that a variety of fundamental factors such as the popularity of the incumbent president and the success of the economy are highly predictive of the eventual outcome of the election.[2]

Economic measures are thought to be important for understanding election outcomes because the party that holds the presidency is generally held responsible for economic conditions in the country. When the economy is doing well, voters tend to reward the party in control by reelecting their candidates to office; but when the economy is doing poorly, voters tend to punish the incumbent party. For example, in 2008, Republican candidate John McCain faced a very difficult electoral environment largely because an economic crisis had begun earlier that year while another Republican—George W. Bush—still held office. As economic conditions continued to deteriorate during that election, Republicans largely took the blame, and this made McCain's pursuit of the White House an uphill battle. He ultimately lost the national popular vote to Barack Obama by 7 points, and Obama carried 365 electoral votes on his way to a landslide victory.

In 2012, the nature of economic conditions was not quite as clear. While the economy had been steadily improving since Obama's first year in office, the unemployment rate was still relatively high at the beginning of that year. Nonetheless, Obama received enough credit for the improvements in the economy to help him edge past Republican nominee Mitt Romney by about 4 percentage points.

By 2016, economic conditions were more clearly improved compared to what they had been in 2012. The unemployment rate had settled around 5 percent, the lowest it had been since early 2008. Other economic measures, such as gross domestic product growth, were also generally strong, if not spectacular. Many in the public also viewed their own economic situations in a favorable light. A Pew Research Center poll conducted in October 2016 found that about half of Americans rated their personal financial situations as either good or excellent.[3] This was the highest level of satisfaction with personal finances since early 2008, before the Great Recession began.

Interestingly, political scientists have found that vote choices are generally more influenced by the direction in which economic conditions are heading rather than by the overall conditions themselves. In other words, the unemployment rate is generally not a good predictor of how presidential elections will turn out, but the more recent changes in the unemployment rate are more influential. Figure 1 shows the relationship between changes in the unemployment rate during the year before each election since 1952 and the incumbent party's share of the two-party vote in those elections. The line in the plot shows a strong trend that when the unemployment rate is increasing in the twelve months leading up to the election, the incumbent party tends to receive a lower percentage of the vote; but when the unemployment rate is dropping, the incumbent party performs better. In 2016, the unemployment rate had dropped by 0.3 percentage points from where it had been at the same time in 2015. Based on previous patterns, this meant that Clinton should win about 51 percent of the two-party vote. As of our writing of this supplement, she had actually received 50.9 percent of the two-party vote. Thus, the election results were very much in line with what we might have expected from standard economic indicators.

Even as economic conditions improved markedly during Obama's second term, Obama did not enjoy a significant boost in his approval rating as a result. A president's approval rating is the percentage of Americans who say that they approve of the job he is doing as president. When presidents enjoy higher approval ratings, their parties tend to perform better in elections. For example, in 1988, George H. W. Bush won the presidency partly because approval of Ronald Reagan was above 50 percent. In 2000, Al Gore won the national popular vote (though not the presidency) thanks in part to outgoing President Bill Clinton's nearly 60 percent approval rating. In 2008, John

FIGURE 1
The Relationship between Change in Unemployment and the Incumbent Party's Share of the Two-Party Vote for President

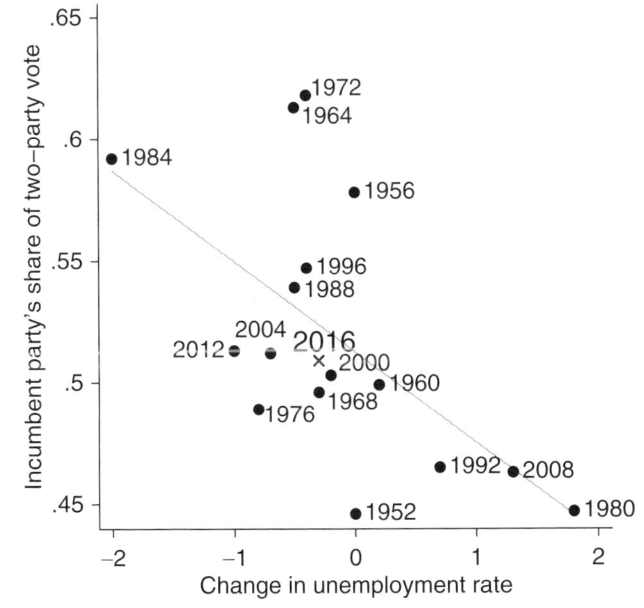

Note: Figure created by authors using data from the Federal Reserve. X-axis shows change in unemployment rate from 3rd quarter of year preceding election to 3rd quarter of the election year. Y-axis is proportion of the vote for the major party candidates received by the candidate from the party that held the White House.

McCain struggled against Barack Obama because of President George W. Bush's very low 25% approval rating. As 2016 began, Obama's approval rating steadily hovered just below 50 percent. He was less popular than Clinton in 2000, but much more popular than Bush had been in 2008.

In short, Obama was popular enough and the economy was strong enough to give a Democratic candidate for president a reasonable shot at winning in 2016, but Obama was not so popular that this would be an easy victory for the Democrats. Adding to the challenge for Democrats was the fact that a third factor also tends to play a role in presidential elections—voters tend to not return the same party to the White House for three consecutive terms. Indeed, since Harry Truman won re-election in 1948 there has only been one instance when presidents from the same party won the presidency in three consecutive elections (Republicans did so in 1980, 1984, and 1988). This pattern likely arises because voters develop a desire for change over time, and also because a party's supporters may become complacent when their party wins several elections in a row. Thus, Democrats were also facing the challenge of trying to retain control of the White House for a rare third consecutive term.

Choosing the Presidential Nominees

The balance of the fundamentals heading into the 2016 presidential campaign suggested a contest that could go either way. Some political science models indicated that Democrats would win a narrow victory in the national popular vote, while other models suggested a narrow advantage for Republicans. Nearly every model indicated that it would be a very close contest.[4] Thus, political scientists expected that 2016 would produce a tight contest for the White House; and given that fact, one thing that was likely to matter was who the parties would nominate to run for the presidency.

The Invisible Primary

Political parties select their presidential nominees through a lengthy and arduous process that begins with the so-called "invisible primary." During the invisible primary, candidates maneuver to set themselves up for success in the actual primaries and caucuses held in the states during the first several months of an election year. Those primaries and caucuses are where candidates attempt to accumulate a majority of convention delegates in order to secure their party's nomination. But success in the invisible primary generally comes by raising large sums of campaign funds from donors, performing well in the preelection polls, and lining up endorsements from party officials. A candidate who is able to accomplish these things should have sufficient name recognition and public support to perform well in early primaries and caucuses and the financial support necessary to sustain that early success over a long nomination campaign on his or her way to becoming the party's nominee.

While candidates jockey for position during the invisible primary, the leaders of each party generally attempt to influence the nomination process to ensure that the strongest candidate will win the nomination and represent the party in the general election campaign. This theory about the role that party elites play in the nomination processes is generally called "The Party Decides," after the name of the influential book that describes the theory.[5] Essentially, the argument is that activists, politicians, and other central players in each party tend to line up their support behind the candidate who they think would run the strongest general election campaign. In past elections, when these party leaders rallied behind a favored candidate by endorsing that candidate during the invisible primary, the favored candidate has usually prevailed in winning the nomination. For Republicans, this pattern has held in every election at least as far back as 1980. A notable exception for Democrats was 2008, when Hillary Clinton held a wide lead in endorsements over Barack Obama before the contests began but ultimately lost the nomination to him. In 2016, it was on the Republican side where the theory would once again fall short.

ROBYN BECK/AFP/Getty Images

Hillary Clinton's success in the Democratic primaries was in many ways a textbook example of "The Party Decides" theory, but it was not without underlying tensions. Here, for example, delegates from the party's left wing hold up signs critical of Clinton at the Democratic National Convention in July 2016: one of several protests against the frontrunner, who was widely seen as representative of the party's "establishment" during a heavily antiestablishment election.

The Democratic Party Decides on Clinton

The 2016 contest for the Democratic Party's nomination was, in many ways, a textbook example of the importance of the invisible primary and the role of party elites in helping to steer the nomination process. Hillary Clinton entered the race as the early front-runner, just as she had in 2008 before she lost to Barack Obama's insurgent candidacy. Almost as soon as she formally announced her candidacy in April 2015, Clinton had a mountain of endorsements from Democratic Party activists and elected officials. She also raised tremendous sums of money; before 2016 even began, Clinton had already raised over $110 million for her campaign.

Clinton's overwhelming support among party leaders did not mean that she would easily claim the party's nomination, however. As she had in 2008, she faced another difficult challenge from an insurgent candidate—this time Vermont Senator Bernie Sanders. Sanders slowly gained ground on Clinton in the national polls during 2015, based largely on his appeal as the antiestablishment candidate. Indeed, Sanders was not actually a member of the Democratic Party at all. In Vermont, he ran for Senate as an independent; although once in the Senate, he generally voted along with the Democrats in Congress. Sanders' liberal populist platform helped him to attract support outside the mainstream of the party and especially among younger Democrats. His viability as a challenger to Clinton was established by his ability to raise over $70 million during 2015 and by his success in the national polls, in which he received increasingly more support throughout the year leading up to the first contests in Iowa and New Hampshire. On the eve of the Iowa caucuses, Sanders still trailed Clinton by more than 10 points in the national polls, but polling indicated that he was tied with Clinton in Iowa and was leading her in New Hampshire, where the first primary would happen one week later.

In 2008, Clinton lost the Iowa caucuses to Obama, a result that helped prove Obama's viability as a candidate and suggested the vulnerability of Clinton's front-runner status. This time, Clinton was able to hold on to defeat Sanders in Iowa—a fact that was especially important given that she was defeated handily by Sanders a week later in the New Hampshire primary. The split results in the two early states did little to separate the two candidates, ensuring that the campaign would extend into the spring and beyond. Both Clinton and Sanders had strengths that allowed them to do exceptionally well in some states, but quite poorly in others. For example, Sanders generally won huge margins among young voters (often receiving more than 80 percent of the vote among primary voters who were 18 to 29 years of age) and also did well among white liberal voters. Clinton typically fared better among older voters (especially women) and minorities like African Americans and Latinos.

Sanders' inability to make inroads with minority voters ultimately kept him from accumulating the number of delegates he would need to win the nomination. Clinton routinely received support from over 80 percent of black voters and between two-thirds and three-fourths of Latinos. This helped to offset the fact that she often trailed Sanders among whites. What made this particularly problematic for Sanders was that in many states, especially in the South, a majority of those voting in the Democratic primaries were nonwhite. Figure 2 shows just how significant this issue was. The x-axis of the figure shows the percentage of Democratic primary or caucus voters in each state who were white while the y-axis shows the percentage of the vote Sanders won in that state's caucus or primary. There was a very strong relationship—for every 1 percentage point decrease in the share of white voters in a state, Sanders generally performed about two-thirds of a point worse in terms of the final vote share. This led him to do particularly poorly in states like Mississippi, Alabama, South Carolina, Georgia, Arkansas, Tennessee, Florida, Texas, and Maryland, where he received 33% or less of the vote.

On the strength of her showing among minority voters and by performing well enough among white Democrats, Clinton was able to build a small but clear edge in the pledged delegates who would formally choose the party's nominee at the convention in July. Adding to her margin of victory were the so-called "super delegates"—party leaders and elected officials who also receive votes at the convention. While it was clear that Clinton would win the nomination, many Sanders supporters continued to protest the outcome, even as the Democratic National Convention began. The protests worried party leaders, who understood the importance of unifying the party

FIGURE 2
Percent of Democratic Primary Electorate Who Were White and Support for Sanders in 2016

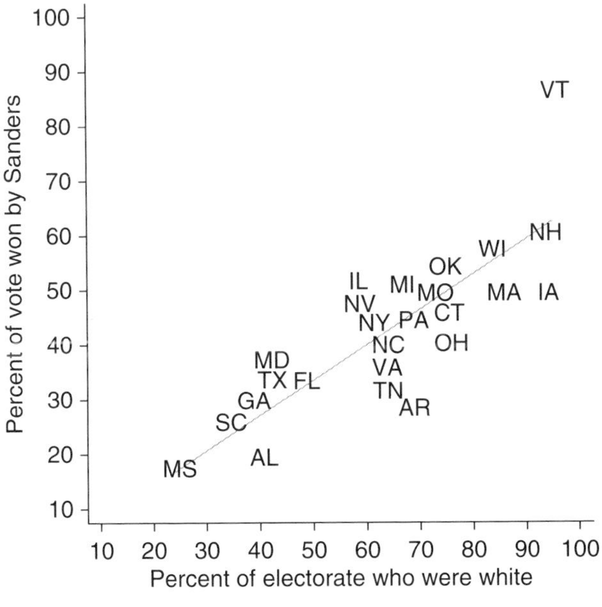

Note: Figure created by authors using data from exit polls compiled by Ariel Edwards-Levy. Figure includes only states where exit polls were conducted.

before the general election campaign began. Ultimately, such unity was mostly achieved, thanks in part to Sanders lending his full endorsement and support for Clinton at the convention and asking his supporters to follow suit.

On July 26, Hillary Clinton officially received the Democratic Party's nomination for president, becoming the first woman to run for president as a nominee of one of the two major parties. The achievement was a testament to Clinton's perseverance and skill during her career in politics, but it also meant that both implicitly and explicitly, gender would be a defining feature of the general election campaign.

The Republican Party Decides Not to Decide

While "The Party Decides" theory did a good job of explaining how the Democratic nomination campaign played out, it fell far short in explaining what happened for Republicans. The nomination of Donald Trump was hardly what Republican Party leaders wanted, and many could not even tolerate it. His ascension to the top during the nomination campaign flew directly in the face of what the authors of *The Party Decides* would have anticipated. At the same time, Trump's success also helped to demonstrate the importance of this theory. Trump prevailed not because the party decided on him as its nominee, but rather because the party failed to decide on anyone as its nominee. By failing to back any viable alternative to Trump, party leaders made his path to the nomination much easier.

On the eve of the first contest—the February 1 Iowa caucuses—Trump had not been endorsed by a single governor or member of Congress. By comparison, Jeb Bush had lined up at least 30 such endorsements, Marco Rubio had more than two dozen, and Ted Cruz had more than a dozen national elected officials backing him. But even these totals were paltry compared to previous nomination races. For example, during the invisible primary in 2012, Romney had secured more endorsements on his own than the entire field had received before the Iowa caucuses in 2016. Thus, it was clear that the Republican establishment was not throwing its collective weight behind any particular candidate before the primaries and caucuses began, but it was also clear that Trump was not the preferred candidate of anyone in the party establishment. A lack of party support for Trump was not particularly surprising. Trump had not been an active member of the Republican Party until recently; and, as he had no experience in elected office, he had not built ties with Republican activists and elected officials. He had, in fact, frequently been an outspoken critic of the party and Republican officeholders, a pattern that made him an even less desirable nominee for the party.

Thus, if "The Party Decides" thesis was correct, Trump's attempt to become the Republican Party's nominee would not be met with success. Elites would line up their endorsements behind another candidate and work to ensure that person would become the nominee instead. They would do this in order to ensure that Republicans put forward the strongest nominee in the general election campaign, as well as someone who would work in cooperation with the party. But this did not happen. While some Republican elected officials did endorse alternative candidates like Bush, Rubio, and Cruz early in the process, the number of endorsements being made was not

Chip Somodevilla/Getty Images

Donald Trump, in contrast to Clinton, won the Republican nomination with a notable lack of endorsement from party elites, and despite frequent breaches in decorum: including his unusually combative debate manner, seen here in the first Republican debate with Wisconsin governor Scott Walker and former Florida governor Jeb Bush.

particularly large compared to previous election cycles. In 2016, it appeared as though the party was deciding not to decide.

Why would Republican Party elites not want to influence the outcome of the nomination process in 2016? One possibility is that there was no real agreement on who the best nominee would be. Jeb Bush was a member of the party's traditional wing, not surprising given the fact that his father and brother were the previous two Republicans to serve in the White House. But the traditional wing of the party had been under attack from movements like the Tea Party, whose members desired a less compromising form of conservatism from their leaders. These antiestablishment Republicans were united in their distaste for Bush, but they were divided or noncommittal in their support for other candidates like Marco Rubio or Ted Cruz. The Republican Party was struggling to identify a single candidate to support for the same reason that Republican Speaker John Boehner had resigned in September 2015—the party elites were not all that unified. Making things even more difficult was the fact that the field of Republicans competing for the nomination was historically large, growing to sixteen candidates at one point. In such a crowded field, it was difficult for party elites to settle on any single potential nominee.

In some ways, this was the perfect setup for a candidacy like Trump's to thrive. With a very large field of candidates and the absence of any concerted effort by

Republican elites to rally around a particular candidate, the field was essentially wide open to anyone who could build momentum by energizing even a relatively small group of supporters.[6]

Trump entered the race for president in June 2015 and immediately vaulted ahead of his competition in the national polls. He did this despite the fact that he sparked a string of controversies with remarks he made during campaign speeches or tweets he sent out at various times during the campaign. For example, when discussing Mexican immigrants at his presidential announcement speech he said: "They're bringing drugs. They're bringing crime. They're rapists. And some, I assume, are good people." The remarks caused the NBC television network to sever ties with Trump, whose television show *The Apprentice* had aired on the network for many years. In December, Trump again sparked outrage by proposing that the United States ban the immigration of all Muslim people into the country. He also frequently created controversy by insulting fellow Republicans. For example, in July, Trump said that former prisoner of war and current Arizona Senator John McCain was not a war hero because "I like people who weren't captured." In September, Trump referred to Republican Carly Fiorina's candidacy by responding, "Look at that face! Would anyone vote for that?"[7] And during the debates in late 2015 and early 2016, he took to calling competitors for the nomination names like "Little Marco (Rubio)" and "Lyin' Ted (Cruz)."

Trump's remarks were unconventional for two main reasons. First, it is unusual for candidates to so frequently target minority groups and public figures for such direct criticism. Typically, politicians attempt to make their criticisms of people and groups more implicitly, so that they can avoid criticism for stepping over a line of decorum.[8] But Trump was unusually direct. Second, Trump rarely apologized for these remarks. Indeed, he often repeated the critiques when asked about them and refused to reframe what he said or meant. Trump's tendency to be direct and uncompromising in comments such as these not only was unusual, but also appeared to be part of what attracted a certain bloc of Republican voters to his campaign. These voters frequently cited Trump's "straight talk" as a trait that set him apart from the other traditional politicians running for office. Thus, while political reporters and pundits continued to think that Trump would ultimately be forced out of the race because of his constant penchant for creating controversy, he steadily continued to lead the pack of candidates for the Republican nomination with about one-third of all Republicans supporting him.

The key question, then, was whether Trump's popularity among about one-third of voters nationwide would translate into victories in early states like Iowa, New Hampshire, and South Carolina, which would then set the tone for the rest of the nomination race. And on February 1, Trump was dealt a blow to his front-runner status when Texas Republican Senator Ted Cruz narrowly won the Iowa caucuses. Cruz's victory in Iowa showed the importance of having a strong campaign organization to contact supporters and get them to turn out. While Trump was performing well in the polls, he put little investment into traditional campaign operations that involved targeting likely supporters and attempting to mobilize them to vote. Cruz, on the other hand, relied on a much more sophisticated "ground game" to ensure that his supporters turned out. This strategy served him particularly well in Iowa, given that the caucuses—which consist of a lengthy meeting before voting is conducted—require a much greater investment of time than simply voting.

However, Cruz's win in the Iowa caucuses was narrow, and he was not particularly well liked by the party establishment either. Thus, rather than coalesce behind Cruz as the best chance to derail a Trump nomination, most party leaders continued to sit on the sidelines, refusing to endorse any candidate in the race. A week later, Trump won the New Hampshire primary easily with 35% of the vote. Second place went to Ohio Governor John Kasich with just 16% of the vote; Cruz, Rubio, and Bush all failed to get more than 12%. Following the New Hampshire primary, the Republican field began to quickly winnow down from the twelve major candidates who competed in the Iowa caucuses to just six candidates who would compete in the South Carolina primary on February 20. Winnowing generally happens when candidates leave the race because they are running out of campaign funds and have not fared well in early contests. With such a large field in 2016, it was always likely to be the case that winnowing would happen quickly, since candidates like Chris Christie, Carly Fiorina, Ben Carson, and others were unable to attract even 10 percent of the vote in the first two contests.

On February 20, Trump won the South Carolina primary with 33% of the vote. But the big story from that evening was that Jeb Bush, who had been viewed as the favorite to win the Republican nomination for much of the invisible primary, withdrew from the race following weak showings in all three early states. With the field now down to four major candidates—Trump, Cruz, Kasich, and Rubio—many believed that Trump would begin to struggle, as there would be fewer candidates to divide the anti-Trump vote. That theory was put to the test for the first time on March 1 (Super Tuesday) when eleven states held primaries and caucuses all on the same date. However, Trump's momentum hardly faltered. He won seven of the eleven contests, while Cruz won three states, and Rubio won in Minnesota. Rubio would drop out of the race two weeks later when he failed to win his home state of Florida. This left just Cruz and Kasich to challenge Trump for the nomination. While Kasich won Ohio and Cruz won several other states, Trump still managed to win most of the primaries and caucuses that remained and was able to accumulate enough delegates to clinch the nomination on May 24.

Even as Trump had enough delegates to secure the Republican nomination, many Republican Party leaders continued to explore ways they might be able to keep him from actually becoming the nominee through procedural moves at the Republican National Convention in July. But just as the party's leaders failed to decide on an alternative candidate to support in opposition to Trump early in the nomination race, they also failed to stop his nomination at the convention. For many Republican leaders, the prospect of upsetting the large share of Republican voters who had supported Trump in the primaries and caucuses was simply too worrisome to face. Thus, on July 19, Donald Trump officially became the Republican Party's candidate for president.

Trump's nomination countered much of what political scientists had typically understood about how party nominations work. Trump won the nomination despite the fact that he had little or no support from leaders and elected officials in the party. In fact, many party leaders actively worked to stop him from receiving the nomination. And he won despite the fact that he focused very little effort on raising money or creating a campaign organization to help him mobilize voters in early primary and caucus states like New Hampshire, Iowa, and South Carolina. Trump lagged far behind several of his primary opponents in fundraising—as of early 2016, Jeb Bush, Marco Rubio, and Ted Cruz had all raised more than twice as much money as Trump. Instead, Trump won largely based on his ability to receive much more coverage in news outlets than his competitors and because his message resonated with a significant share of the Republican electorate. Of course, many political scientists doubted that Trump's success would continue into the general election campaign; once again, they would be wrong.

The General Election Campaign

Political scientists often debate whether campaigns matter much when it comes to determining who wins presidential elections. As we noted earlier, fundamentals such as economic performance and presidential approval are strongly related to the eventual election outcomes, raising questions about how much of a difference the

Justin Sullivan/Getty Images

Hillary Clinton, shown here campaigning in Michigan on the day before the election, ran a polished, streamlined, and well-funded campaign; but it was not enough to overcome the highly unfavorable opinions of many voters.

campaign could really make. But if a general election campaign was ever going to matter in determining the outcome of a presidential election, 2016 seemed to be the year in which that would happen. But how important was the campaign in the end?

The Case for Thinking the Campaign Mattered

Once the party nominees were determined, many political scientists expected that 2016 would be the year when the campaign would be more influential than ever. One reason for this was the imbalance in the quality of the nominees of the two parties. One nominee was a political novice who had never run for nor held any position in government, while the other was one of the most qualified individuals to ever run for president in terms of experience in various public service roles. Adding to this imbalance in the political experience of the candidates were the funds each had raised for competing in the general election and the professionalism of their campaign organizations more generally. The Clinton campaign and her affiliated organizations raised well over $1 billion during the election cycle, while Trump and his affiliated campaign organizations raised only about half as much. Similarly, the Clinton campaign maintained more than twice as many campaign offices nationally as Trump's campaign did.[9] No recent presidential campaign had produced such a lopsided array of campaign resources as did that of 2016.

The 2016 general election campaign was also unique in terms of Americans' overwhelmingly negative views of the candidates running. As Figure 3 shows, both Clinton and Trump entered the general election campaign as the most disliked nominees since Gallup began collecting such data from its polls in 1956. One-third of American adults had a highly unfavorable opinion of Hillary Clinton when Gallup conducted its poll in June. By comparison, just 24% of Americans held a highly unfavorable view of Barack Obama when he ran for reelection just four years earlier. As unpopular as Clinton was, Trump was disliked even more. Over 40 percent of Americans held a highly unfavorable view of Trump in June, making him about twice as unpopular as other recent Republican nominees such as Mitt Romney, John McCain, and George W. Bush.

Because of this unprecedented unpopularity, many voters responded to preelection polls by stating that they intended to vote for third-party candidates or that they were not yet sure for whom they planned to vote. According to pollster.com, by September 1, the average national polling found that 11.9% of voters said that they would vote for someone other than Trump or Clinton while 6.4% were undecided. By comparison, in 2012, only 8.5% of voters said they planned to vote for someone other than Obama or Romney, and just 5.4% were undecided. Given that nearly one-in-five likely voters had not committed to a major party candidate two months before the election, there was certainly potential for the campaign to influence the outcome.

Figure 4 shows how Clinton and Trump fared in the national polls between September 1 and the election on November 8. The shaded areas in the plot essentially account for sampling error and constitute a range within which each candidate's

FIGURE 3
Percent of Americans Giving Highly Unfavorable Ratings to Presidential Nominees, 1956–2016

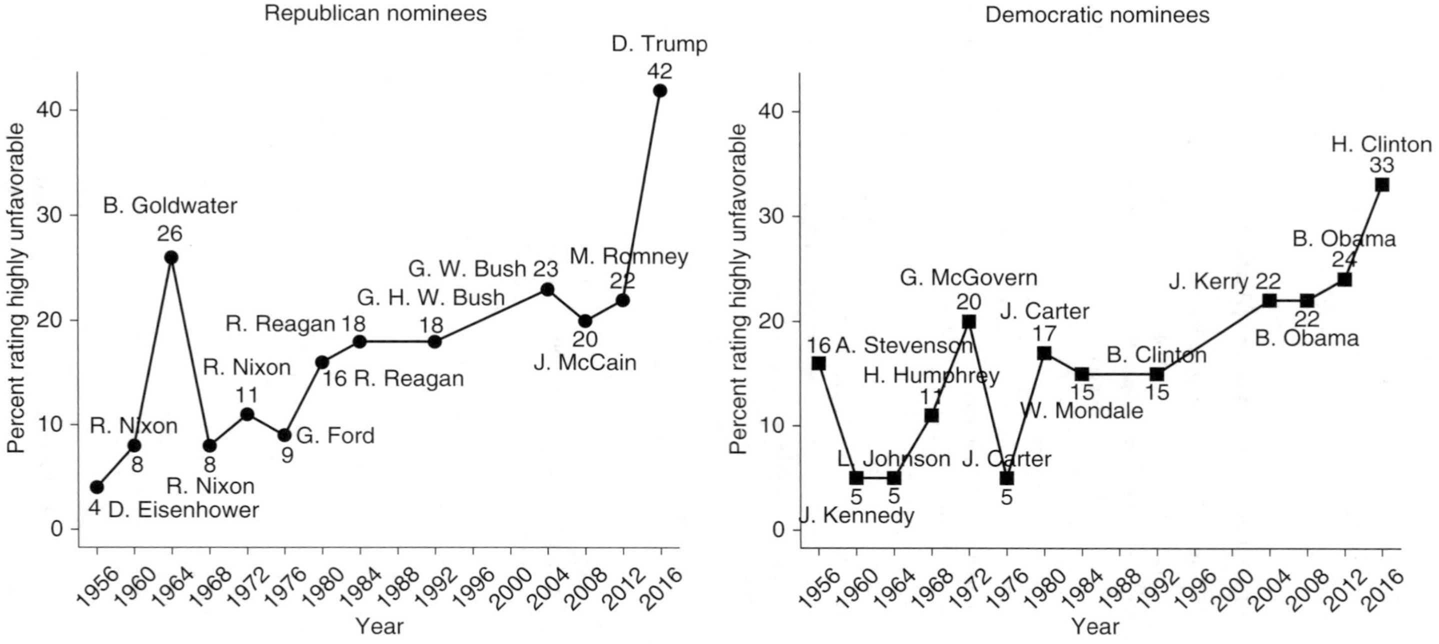

Note: Figure created by authors using data retrieved from http://www.gallup.com/poll/193376/trump-leads-clinton-historically-bad-image-ratings.aspx

support was likely to be. The figure also denotes key points during the campaign. The televised debates are often the most important campaign events during the months preceding the election.[10] They act as focal events during which a large number of likely voters see the candidates in action and assess their performances. The news coverage that follows the debates is often even more influential, as people tend to read about how one candidate fared better than the other, which might also influence their vote decisions. Generally speaking, however, the most influential debate is the first debate, since it provides the first such opportunity to watch the candidates engage with each other one-on-one.

In 2016, the first debate did appear to be influential. In the wake of the debate, Clinton saw an uptick in her support while Trump's support dropped below 40 percent. This downward trend for Trump was only further reinforced right before the second debate when a tape was released from the television show *Access Hollywood* that captured Trump making very lewd remarks about how he had engaged in behavior that would legally be considered sexual assault. When the tape was released, many Republican elected officials announced that they would no longer support Trump's campaign for president, and many in the party began to fear

FIGURE 4
Average Support for Clinton and Trump in Polls Conducted from September 1 Through Election Day

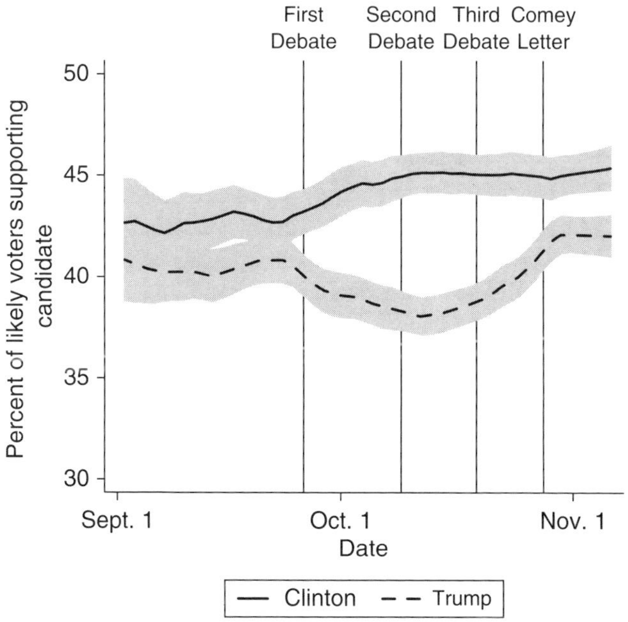

Note: Figure created by authors using data retrieved from pollster.com. Graph shows smoothed average support for candidates with 95% confidence intervals.

that Clinton and the Democrats were headed for a landslide victory. Trump's support, however, bottomed out in mid-October and began to increase again as the election grew closer. With a week left in the campaign, Trump was at a slightly higher level of support than he had been back in September, though he still trailed Clinton by 3 to 4 points in the national polls.

The Case for Thinking the Campaign Was of Minimal Importance

One way to interpret Figure 4 is to see the first debate as a campaign event that was clearly influential. However, another interpretation of the figure might be to see the limitations of campaign events. After all, Trump's support did temporarily drop in the wake of the first debate and the release of the *Access Hollywood* tape, but it ultimately rebounded to where it had been by early November. On the other side, the Clinton campaign argued that they had been negatively affected by the release of a letter from FBI Director James Comey announcing that he was reopening an investigation into Clinton's emails from when she served as Secretary of State. Yet, the figure seems to indicate that the Comey letter did little to affect support for Clinton in the polls.

One reason to expect that campaigns may be of little importance is because of the increasing partisan polarization in the electorate that has occurred in the past few decades.[11] Citizens are now much less likely than they were in the past to vote for candidates of the opposite party. This is partly a matter of preference—citizens who have committed to being Republicans or Democrats have stated a particular interest in supporting candidates from those parties, so that they do so nine out of ten times is not surprising. But what makes partisanship even more influential is that it also structures how citizens engage with the political world and how they process new information that they encounter every day. As such, it can serve to dramatically limit the influence of campaign events.

Scholars who study political psychology often make note of a phenomenon called partisan motivated reasoning.[12] The idea is that when Republicans or Democrats are confronted with new information, they tend to engage with that information in a way that minimizes the need to reevaluate their political allegiances. If the new information reinforces their beliefs about their party, then they accept the information; but if the new information would challenge those beliefs, they generally dismiss the information or argue against its veracity. For example, scholars have frequently found that people are generally dismissive of good economic news when the president is a member of the opposite party. After all, partisans do not want to have to reevaluate their beliefs that a president from the opposite party might be successful in managing the economy, so they choose instead simply not to believe the economic news. Indeed, partisans often have disparate beliefs about objective facts. In a 2012 survey that asked individuals what they thought the unemployment rate was, Democrats generally gave much more accurate responses than Republicans who gave much higher estimates, on average.[13]

While partisans are often too quick to reject facts that do not fit with their political preferences, they are also often too eager to accept new information that does. For this reason, partisan motivated reasoning can also facilitate the spread of misinformation. This was clear during the Obama presidency when a significant percentage of Republicans believed that Obama was not a citizen, no matter how much evidence was presented to support Obama's citizenship.

If a significant share of the electorate is comprised of partisans who are engaged in motivated reasoning, then there is much less potential for campaigns to matter. After all, people are much less likely to be persuaded to change their partisan allegiances than they are to dismiss or explain away new information that arises during the campaign. So when the *Access Hollywood* tapes surfaced showing Trump engaged in lewd joking about activities that would constitute sexual assault, Republicans largely explained it away as "locker room talk" and not a real reflection on Trump. And when FBI Director Comey announced that he was reopening the investigation into Clinton's emails, Democrats resoundingly attacked the announcement as a partisan ploy without any foundation.

Given this, it should come as no surprise that exit polls showed that 90% of Democrats voted for Clinton and 90% of Republicans voted for Trump.

TIMOTHY A. CLARY/AFP/Getty Images

Despite being the most disliked presidential candidate in decades, Trump still retained the loyalty of 90% of Republicans: an example, arguably, of what scholars of political psychology call partisan motivated reasoning.

As disliked as each candidate was and as much controversial campaign news was made during 2016, Republicans and Democrats voted for their party's nominees at basically the same rate as they had in the previous half-dozen presidential elections.

Campaigns Are Mostly about Mobilization

When one thinks about politics in terms of partisan motivated reasoning, campaign effects are less likely to be related to people changing their minds about who to support. Instead, where campaigns might matter the most is simply in terms of energizing supporters and turning them out to vote at higher numbers than the other campaign.[14] The Clinton campaign was expected to be stronger in this area, at least partly because of the significant investment it was able to make into organizing volunteers and staff to call, text, email, and go door-to-door making sure their supporters turned out to vote. But often the party that has been out of the White House for several terms has an advantage in mobilizing its supporters, who feel more motivated to ensure that their candidate wins.

In the immediate aftermath of an election, it is often difficult to judge how each party fared in terms of mobilizing its supporters. While we know that the overall turnout rate in 2016 was mostly in line with the rate in 2012 (about 59 percent of those who were eligible to vote did so), that does not necessarily tell us whether the electorate favored one party more than the other. The final demographics of the 2016 electorate will only be known several months from the writing of this text, but there were some early signs that in key states, traditional Democratic constituencies were not voting at the same rates as they had in previous years. Several key states make it easy for people to vote early, before election day. In some states, like North Carolina and Florida, more than half of those who voted in 2016 actually voted early.

In Figure 5, we examine how the composition of early voters changed from 2012 to 2016 in key states that provide the data to track this information. Specifically, the graph shows the difference in the share of early voters who were registered Democrats in 2016 compared to 2012. Overall, the figure shows that in 2016 Democrats were lagging behind their mobilization efforts from 2012 in six of the eight states. In swing states like Florida, North Carolina, and Ohio, Democratic turnout in early voting was 3 percentage points lower than it had been in 2012. In states that were sure to be close, this turnout differential could be crucial. And in many states, the Democratic dip in turnout appeared to be because of a drop in early voting among African Americans. For example, in North Carolina, African Americans accounted for 27% of all early voters in 2012, but just 22.7% in 2016.

Thus, despite a clear edge in terms of resources and organization, the Clinton campaign appeared to be falling behind benchmarks established in 2012 when Obama ran for reelection. And while early voting was only part of the turnout story in 2016, it did provide an early sign that Democrats might not be mobilizing enough supporters to win the election.

FIGURE 5
Change in Democratic Share of Early Voters in Eight Key States, 2012–2016

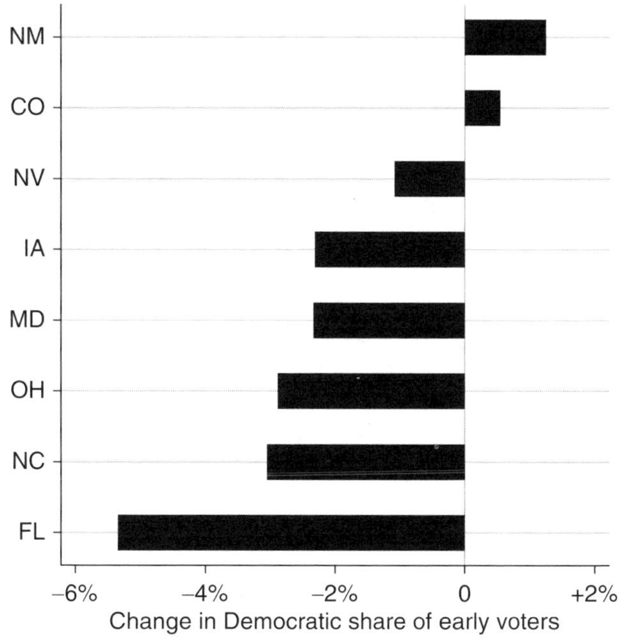

Note: Figure created by authors based on data obtained from Catalist.

The Outcome

As election night approached, it was clear that everyone, including the Trump campaign, expected a Clinton victory. But as the polls closed and the night wore on, states that Clinton expected to carry easily, like Wisconsin, Michigan, and Pennsylvania, were too close to call. And states that Clinton had hoped to win, like Florida, North Carolina, and Ohio, were going to Trump. At around 1:30 a.m. (EST) on November 9, the Associated Press called the state of Pennsylvania for Trump, closing off any path to victory for Clinton, who conceded the election to Trump shortly thereafter. It was a shocking turn of events, surprising nearly everyone. How did it happen?

Another Electoral College/Popular Vote Split

There are many aspects of the 2016 election result that are noteworthy, but one of those is the fact that the candidate who won the most votes was not elected president. Nationally, Clinton received over 2 million more votes than Trump, meaning that she won the popular vote by at least 1.5 percentage points. Yet, the fact that votes are

Win McNamee/Getty Images

Trump's electoral college victory was a historic upset, going against the predictions of all major polls. Here, a supporter of Hillary Clinton reacts in shock at the candidate's election night event in New York City.

tallied and allocated state-by-state through the Electoral College means that small states receive more influence in determining who wins the presidency.

Figure 6 shows the advantage (or disadvantage) that the Democratic presidential candidates won in the popular vote compared to the advantage they won in the Electoral College in each election since 1992. One point that has always been true about the Electoral College is that it tends to magnify the margin of the winner's victory since most states allocate their electoral votes in a winner-take-all format. This pattern can be seen in 1992, 1996, 2004, 2008, and 2012. But note that the Electoral College has put Democrats at a disadvantage twice since the turn of the century. In 2000, Al Gore narrowly lost in the Electoral College (by 1 percentage point) despite narrowly winning the popular vote (by 0.5 point). Before 2000, such a split between the popular vote and Electoral College had not happened since 1888. But in 2016 the difference between the popular vote and Electoral College tally was even more striking. Trump won a 13.8% advantage in Electoral College votes despite the fact that Clinton won the popular vote by 2.1 points. Thus, Trump would become the second Republican president to take office since 2000 despite having more Americans vote for his opponent than for him.

This context is important for several reasons. First, it is important not to overstate the meaning of Trump's victory. After all, Clinton won millions more votes than Trump nationally. In fact, 2016 was the sixth time in the past seven presidential

FIGURE 6
Percent Popular and Electoral College Votes for Democratic Candidate Minus Republican Candidate, 1992–2016

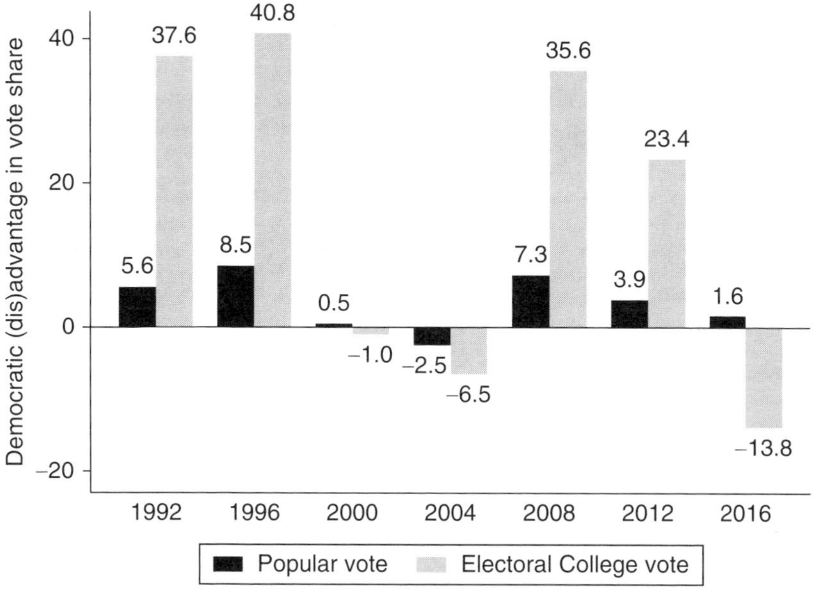

Note: Figure created by authors using data from http://uselectionatlas.org

elections when the Democratic candidate for president won more votes than the Republican. The 2004 election was the only instance during this period when a Republican presidential candidate won more votes than the Democrat. Thus, Democrats' failure in 2016 was perhaps more a matter of how their supporters are distributed geographically than anything else. If a few million people moved from California and New York to Wisconsin, Michigan, and Pennsylvania, the narrative of the 2016 election would be quite different.

Second, the fact that Trump lost the popular vote by a fairly significant margin would also mean that his claim for a mandate in office was more tenuous. After all, a clear majority voted against his candidacy and his policies. This fact, combined with the large share of the public who continued to hold negative views of him even after the election meant that it would be difficult for him to claim widespread public support for his presidency. We return to this point in the conclusion.

Where the Election Was Won

In 2012, Barack Obama won the popular vote by a 4-point margin over Mitt Romney (51% to 47%). In 2016, Clinton's popular vote margin over Trump was a little less than 2 percentage points (48% to 46%). If Clinton's margin had uniformly been

2 points lower than Obama's in each state, she would have won the Electoral College. After all, in 2012, Obama won Pennsylvania by a 5-point margin over Romney, Wisconsin by a 7-point margin, and Michigan by 10 points. Even if you subtract 2 points from each of those margins, Clinton would still have prevailed. Most of the preelection polling in these states had also shown a fairly safe margin for Clinton, generally finding her up by 5 or 6 points over Trump. These states were viewed as Clinton's so-called "firewall"; the view was that she could count on these states to push her to victory even if she lost other more competitive states like Ohio, Florida, and North Carolina.

However, as Figure 7 shows, Clinton lost much more ground in some states than in others; and in a few places she actually performed better than Obama. In states like New Mexico, Florida, and North Carolina, Clinton's vote was about 2 percentage points worse than Obama's, mirroring what happened nationally. However, she performed about 7 points worse than Obama in Pennsylvania, 8 points worse than Obama in

FIGURE 7
Change in Democratic Candidate's Margin over Republican Candidate in Key States, 2012–2016

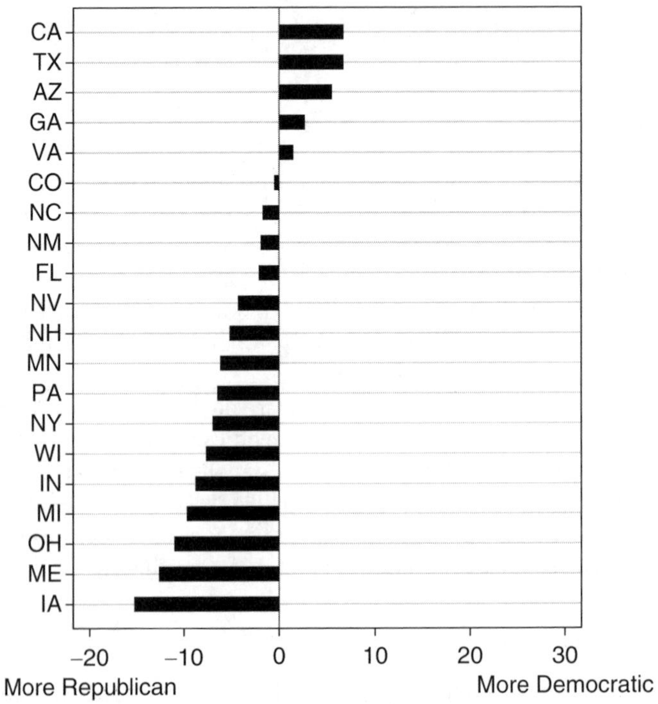

Note: Figure created by authors. X-axis plots the difference between Clinton's margin over Trump in 2016 and Obama's margin over Romney in 2012.

Wisconsin, 10 points worse in Michigan, 11 points worse in Ohio, and 15 points worse in Iowa. In other words, Clinton drastically underperformed relative to Obama in the Midwest. At the same time, Clinton actually did better than Obama in states like Virginia, Georgia, Arizona, Texas, and California. Indeed, it was largely because of Clinton's strong performance in the two largest states—California and Texas—that she was able to win the popular vote even while Trump performed so well in the Midwest.

The vote swing in the Midwest and in other parts of the country appeared to largely follow an urban-rural divide. Clinton won America's 100 most populated (urban) counties by a margin of about 13 million votes over Trump. But Clinton won very few counties beyond those urban areas; in the 3,000 or so other counties in the United States, Trump enjoyed a nearly 12 million vote margin over Clinton. Trump won because he performed better than previous Republican nominees in the rural parts of America while Clinton was not able to get as many urban voters to the polls as she needed to in key cities like Philadelphia, Detroit, and Milwaukee.

How Key Groups Voted

One way that political scientists understand election results is by using exit polls to determine how particular groups voted. Exit polls are conducted on the day of the election at voting sites all over the country. Interviewers ask people leaving the polls to answer a brief questionnaire anonymously regarding their vote, their demographics, and their opinions on key issues. These polls have been conducted for decades, providing a useful baseline for judging how groups have changed in their voting behavior over time.

When Democrats have fared well in recent presidential elections, it has typically been on the strength of attracting a coalition of minority groups, such as African Americans and Latinos, while also performing well among women and younger voters. The Democratic candidate's margin among these groups for elections from 1980 to 2016 is plotted in Figure 8. In 2008, Obama won African Americans by a 91-point margin over McCain (95% to 4%) and Latinos by 36 points (67% to 31%). He also performed exceptionally well with 18–29 year olds, winning the group by 34 points, and he won women by 13 points.

In 2016, Clinton performed just as well among Latinos as Obama had in 2008, she performed almost as well among African Americans, and she won a similar share of the women's vote as Obama had in that election. Her support among younger voters, however, was substantially lower. Given that Clinton fared fairly similarly to Obama among the key groups plotted in Figure 8, it raises a question about where she might have lost support to Trump, particularly in terms of groups that would have especially hurt her in the Midwestern states that Democrats carried in recent elections. Republicans have won the white vote in every election since 1980, though the size of that advantage has fluctuated significantly over time. In 1992, George H. W. Bush won whites by just 1 percentage point over Bill Clinton, and Bob Dole won whites by just 3 points in 1996. Republicans lost both elections by wide margins. By contrast, George W. Bush carried the white vote by a 17-point margin over John Kerry in 2004.

FIGURE 8
Democratic Candidate's Margin over Republican Candidate with Key Subgroups, 1980–2016

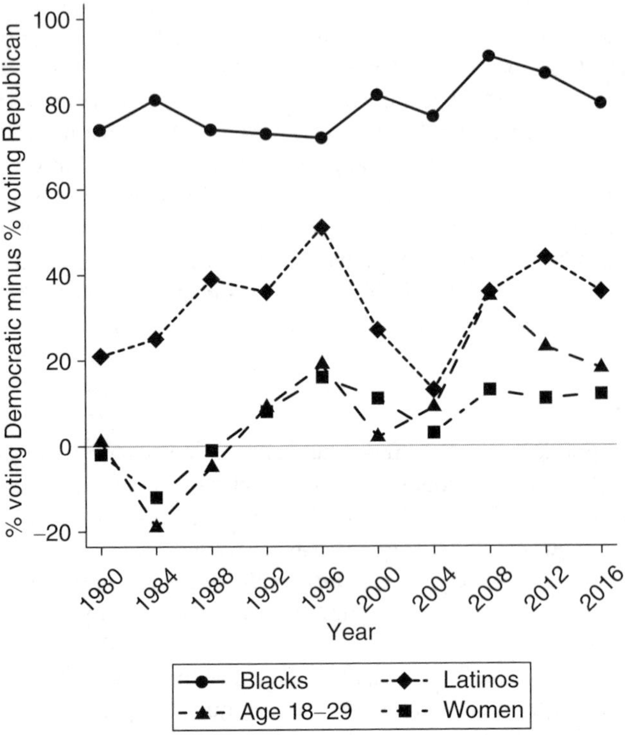

Note: Figure created by the authors using data obtained from the New York Times (http://www.nytimes.com/interactive/2016/11/08/us/politics/election-exit-polls.html). Figure shows percent of each group voting for the Democratic candidate minus percent voting for the Republican candidate.

Obama was able to win easily in 2008 by losing the white vote by "only" 12 points; but according to the exit polls, Clinton lost whites by 21 points in 2016.

But what is especially noteworthy is which white voters she lost. As we noted above, the rural-urban divide in 2016 was larger than in any recent election. And much of this urban-rural divide appears to be related to education.[15] This pattern is especially evident in the exit polls. Figure 9 plots the Democratic margin among whites with and without college degrees from 1980 to 2016. A few patterns are noteworthy here. First, from 1980 to 1996, there was very little difference in how whites voted based on whether they had a college degree. This can be seen from the fact that the lines are closely connected during that period. However, after 1996, we see that the lines began to separate, with non-college-educated whites becoming more Republican in their vote choices from 2000 on. However, even from 2000 through 2012, the lines still move together from year to year. That is, when college-educated whites voted more Democratic from one election to the next, so did non-college-educated whites. Thus, when Obama won in 2008, college-educated whites were far more supportive of him than non-college-educated whites, but both groups voted more Democratic than they had in the previous election.

The 2016 election, however, broke this pattern. College-educated whites were actually more supportive of Clinton in 2016 than they had been of Obama in 2012, but non-college-educated whites moved in the opposite direction, preferring Trump over Clinton by nearly 40 points. Specifically, in 2016, 49% of whites with a college degree voted for Trump while 45% voted for Clinton. By comparison, 67% of whites without a college degree voted for Trump, compared to just 28% for Clinton. This pattern was especially significant in Midwestern states that Obama had won in 2008 and 2012. Non-college-educated whites made up over 40 percent of the electorate in Wisconsin, Michigan, Pennsylvania, and Ohio; and in each state, that group preferred Trump by a substantial two-to-one margin. To be sure, the split among whites with and without college degrees was one of the more striking features of the 2016 election.

FIGURE 9
Democratic Candidate's Margin over Republican Candidate among White Voters Depending on College Degree Status, 1980–2016

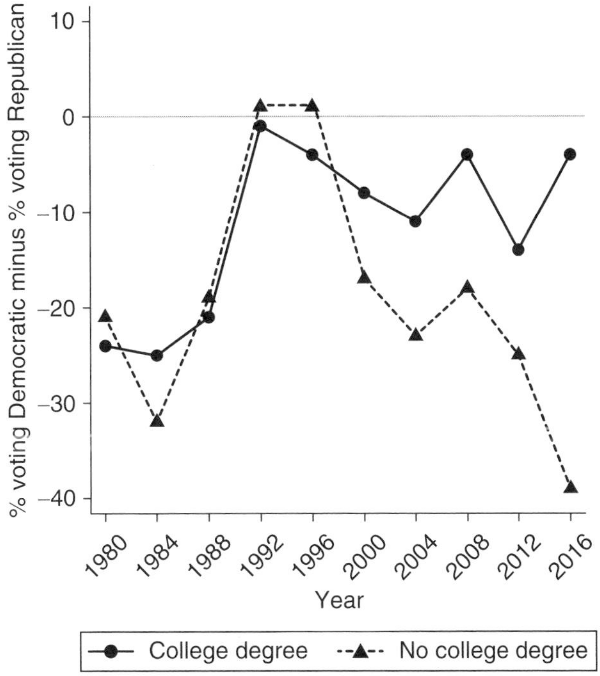

Note: Figure created by the authors using data obtained from the New York Times (http://www.nytimes.com/interactive/2016/11/08/us/politics/election-exit-polls.html). Figure shows percent of whites with and without college degrees voting for the Democratic candidate minus percent voting for the Republican candidate.

Why People Voted for Trump

While exit polls tend to be good indicators of how particular groups vote, they are often less useful in helping to discern why those groups voted the way they did. The reason for this is that they often fail to ask questions that tap into key concepts that might help to explain voting behavior. Thus, explanations for why people favored Trump over Clinton were often just born of speculation. Some argued that Trump's appeal was largely a result of the economic insecurity that many individuals felt and that Trump was able to tap into this insecurity with his populist message. Others argued that it was Trump's antiminority rhetoric during the campaign that helped to galvanize this group behind him by tapping in to the latent racism some of those individuals held. Still others pointed to Trump's sexist behavior on the campaign trail and the fact that the Democratic nominee was a woman to suggest that what drove these voters to support Trump so overwhelmingly was sexism.[16]

Notably, a postelection analysis of factors affecting support for Trump indicates that all of these things mattered to some extent. Using survey data from just before the election, it is possible to control for standard factors such as ideology, partisanship, gender, age, education, and income while testing how much economic dissatisfaction mattered in affecting support for Trump compared to attitudes related to sexism and racism.[17] Figure 10 shows how each of these factors affected the probability that an average white respondent would vote for Trump in 2016. The first plot in the figure shows that as an average respondent moves from being very satisfied with his or her own economic condition to being very dissatisfied, their probability of voting for Trump increased from about .45 to about .6. Thus, economic dissatisfaction was clearly an important factor for white voters in 2016.

The second plot in Figure 10 shows how moving from expressing the least sexist views to the most sexist views would affect the same average respondent's probability of voting for Trump. Specifically, an average white voter who expressed the least sexist attitudes would have just a 40 percent chance of voting for Trump, but the same individual would have a 70 percent chance of voting for Trump if he or she expressed the most sexist attitudes. The third plot in Figure 10 shows a very similar relationship for people who express the least versus most racist views.

Overall, then, economic insecurity appeared to be part of the story for why Trump fared so well, but an even bigger part of the story appeared to be his appeal to those who held more sexist or racist attitudes. When political scientists examined vote preferences in previous elections using similar scales for racism and sexism, they found smaller or nonexistent relationships. With regard to racism, scholars have found that racist attitudes were a stronger predictor of vote choice in 2016 than they were when Obama was running in 2008 and 2012. Political scientist Michael Tessler explains that while Obama rarely discussed racial issues during his campaigns, "Donald Trump repeatedly went where prior Republican presidential candidates were unwilling to go: making explicit appeals to racial resentment, religious intolerance, and white identity."[18] A similar argument can be made about sexism. Of course, gender was always going to be important in an election featuring the first female major

FIGURE 10

Effect of Economic Dissatisfaction, Sexism, and Racism on the Probability of an Average White Voter Supporting Trump

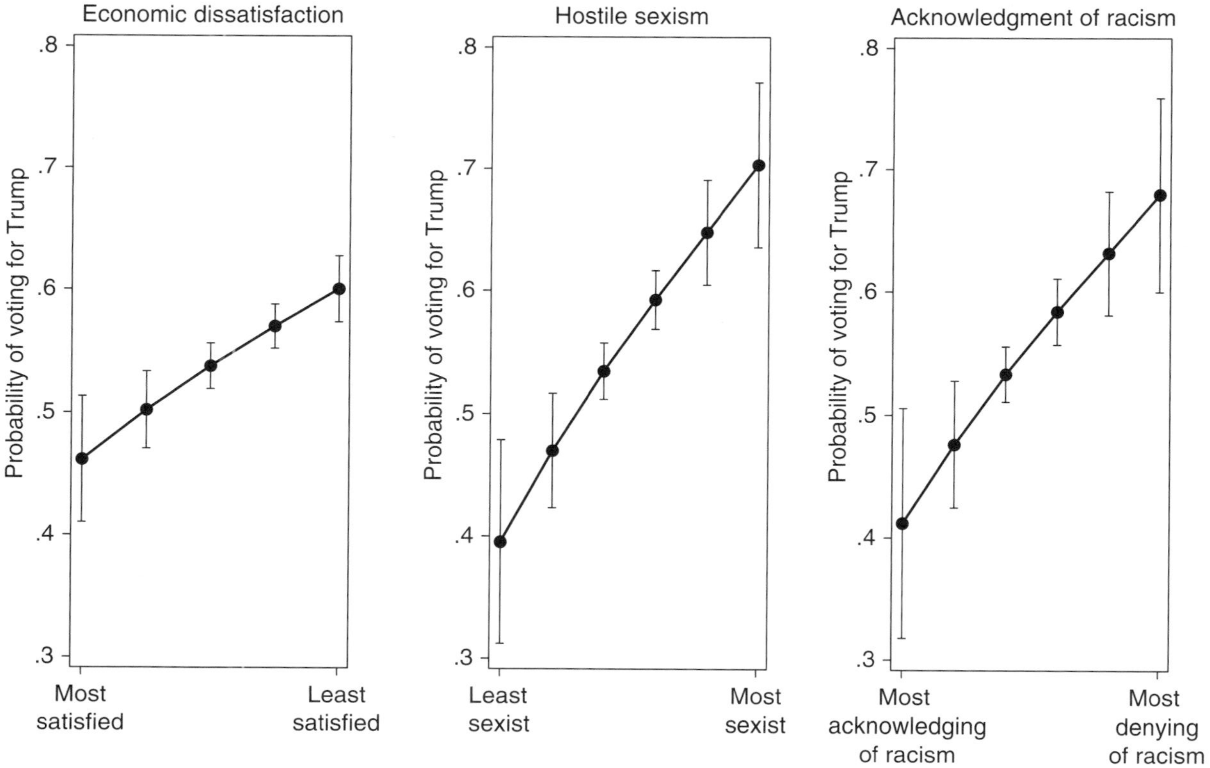

Note: Figure created by authors using data from a national survey conducted by YouGov from October 26–31. Plot shows predicted probability of a respondent voting for Trump (rather than Clinton), holding all other variables at their mean values.

party nominee; but Trump frequently employed sexist rhetoric during the campaign that, combined with sexual assault allegations and the *Access Hollywood* tape, made sexism all the more relevant.

This analysis about why voters supported Trump may also help to explain the education divide that occurred among whites in 2016. In the same survey, whites without a college education tended to score higher on the racism and sexism scales compared to those with college degrees. That is, Trump's rhetoric on race and gender may have led some less educated whites to support him in higher numbers, while some of those with college degrees may have chosen not to support him because of this rhetoric. Importantly, this is not to suggest that all (or even most) of Trump's support resulted from a campaign that activated racial and gender attitudes to an unprecedented degree, but it did seem to explain, at least partially, why some voters were attracted to Trump's candidacy.

The Battle for Control of Congress

Although the race for the presidency captured most of the attention from voters, it was far from the only election in 2016. All seats in the U.S. House of Representatives and one-third of the seats in the U.S. Senate were up for election, too; and the

Zach Gibson/Getty Images

Senator Mitch McConnell (R-KY) addresses the press in Washington, D.C., following the election of Donald Trump as the president of the United States. McConnell retained his position as Senate majority leader, as only two Senate seats were lost to Democrats in the congressional elections.

outcomes of those elections would affect the ability of a new president to carry out his or her agenda. As is often the case, the outcome of most congressional elections was not in doubt. Instead, a handful of seats in each chamber were hotly contested, and the outcome of those races—particularly in the Senate—would determine which party would assume control of the legislative process.

How Republicans Kept the Senate Red

Democrats had high hopes for retaking the Senate in 2016. Going into the election, Republicans held 54 Senate seats to the Democrats 46 (including two independents who caucus with the Democrats). Moreover, Republicans had to defend 24 of the 34 seats in which elections were being held. As the Trump campaign floundered in September and early October, the election forecast looked rosier for Senate Democrats. In order to win majority control, Democrats merely had to retain control of their ten seats and flip five of 24 Republican seats into their column.

The task proved to be too difficult to achieve, however, as Democrats were able to pick up only two additional seats. Ironically, in an election where the Republican presidential candidate ran as an outsider with little support from his party's establishment, voters seemingly paid even more attention than usual to party labels. For the first time since the U.S. Constitution was amended to mandate the direct election of senators, every state that voted Republican for president also elected a Republican senator and every state that voted Democrat for president elected a Democratic senator.[19] Many of the margins of victory were similar for both offices, too. The nationalization of Senate races in 2016 contrasts sharply with recent election cycles where local factors and candidate matchups seemed more important than national trends.

One key issue affecting all Senate races may have its role in the confirmation of Supreme Court justices. When a vacancy occurs on the Court, the President nominates a replacement who then must be approved by the Senate. The death of Justice Antonin Scalia in February 2016 created one such vacancy. The Republican-controlled Senate refused to move on President Obama's nominee to replace Scalia on the bench, claiming that the opportunity to fill the vacancy should wait until the next president is sworn in. With the Court evenly divided, like the country as a whole, the new justice would likely tip the balance in one ideological direction or the other. Controversial issues like abortion rights and marriage equality seemed to hang in the balance.

A second possible explanation for the partisan connection between candidates for president and Senate may simply be the unique nature of the presidential campaign itself. With so much attention focused on the top of the ticket, there was little opportunity for Senate candidates to establish themselves as worthy of election on their own merits.

Senate challengers—at least the successful ones—tend to be experienced campaigners with better name recognition than the typical House challengers. The rate at which incumbent senators win reelection tends to be lower and fluctuates more than for the House, although it is generally quite high. Five senators retired in 2016 (three Democrats and two Republicans), and 27 of the 29 incumbents seeking to retain their seats were successful, yielding a reelection rate of 93%.

Only two incumbent senators, both Republicans, were defeated in 2016. Senator Mark Kirk of Illinois was considered the most vulnerable senator running for reelection. Kirk was first elected in 2010 to the Senate seat previously held by Barack Obama. He suffered a stroke in 2012 and was in recovery for about a year before returning to his Senate duties. His Democratic challenger was Representative Tammy Duckworth, who was elected to the House in 2012. A military veteran, she lost her legs when her helicopter was shot down during the Iraq War. Kirk was already trailing in the polls when he made a statement during a debate that seemed to denigrate Duckworth's ethnicity (she was born in Thailand to a Thai mother and an American father) and military record. He lost by a 54%–40% margin.

The contest in which the other incumbent lost a reelection bid was considerably closer. Like Kirk, New Hampshire Senator Kelly Ayotte was first elected in 2010. She faced criticism during the campaign for first endorsing Donald Trump then backing away in the wake of the *Access Hollywood* recording. She was challenged by Democrat Maggie Hassan, who was in her second term as New Hampshire's governor. The race was so close that the outcome was not determined until the morning after the election. Hassan won by fewer than 1,000 votes out of more than 700,000 cast.

The Democrats' path to taking control of the Senate was buoyed when two former senators came out of retirement to contest seats held by Republicans. In Indiana, Democrat Evan Bayh returned to politics to face Republican Representative Todd Young following the retirement of Senator Dan Coats. Bayh had served two terms as governor and two as senator before retiring in 2010. He was heavily favored in early polling, but his large lead evaporated amid charges that he had lost touch with Indiana voters. Young won by almost 10 percentage points. In Wisconsin, Democrat Russ Feingold squared off in a rematch against Ron Johnson, the Republican who defeated him in 2010. Feingold was favored to win until the end, when Johnson (like Trump) pulled out the win in Wisconsin by a narrow margin.

Most states use partisan primaries to select nominees who subsequently face each other in the general election, but not all do. An unusual contest in California pitted two Democrats in the general election. Under California election law, the primary field consists of all candidates regardless of party affiliation. The top two finishers square off in the general election. A whopping 34 candidates entered the race to succeed retiring Democratic Senator Barbara Boxer. California Attorney General Kamala Harris and Representative Loretta Sanchez placed first and second, respectively, with Harris winning the general election by a margin of almost two-to-one. Louisiana uses a similar process, although the primary takes place on the day of the general election and a runoff is required if no candidate receives a majority in the primary. Twenty-four candidates ran to replace Republican David Vitter, who was retiring from the Senate after an unsuccessful bid for governor in 2015. The top two finishers, Republican John Kennedy and Democrat Foster Campbell, will face one another in a runoff election on December 10. Kennedy is heavily favored, as he and his fellow Republicans together received more than 60 percent of the vote in the primary.

NICHOLAS KAMM/AFP/Getty Images

Congressman Paul Ryan (R-WI) sits beside President-Elect Trump at a postelection press conference in Washington, D.C. Ryan retained his position as Speaker of the House, with a total of only six seats lost to Democrats in the congressional elections.

Assuming a Kennedy win in Louisiana, Republicans will hold a slim 52–48 majority in the Senate. Unlike the House, where a united majority party can enforce its will regardless of its size, Senate rules typically require 60 votes to end debate and approve legislation. Senate Republicans will need to build bipartisan coalitions or resort to extraordinary rule changes to advance their party's agenda.

Why Republicans Retained Their House Majority

While the Senate was seemingly in reach for Democrats heading into the 2016 elections, taking control of House was a more daunting challenge. House Republicans held a 59-seat majority, so Democrats would need a net gain of 30 seats to achieve majority status. Such swings are not unprecedented, as demonstrated by Democrats in 2006 and Republicans in 2010, but they are uncommon. In the end, Republicans lost only six seats, leaving them with a slightly narrowed 241–194 majority when the new congress convenes in 2017.[20]

House incumbents tend to win reelection at even higher rates than their Senate counterparts; more than 85 percent of incumbents running for reelection have been successful in each election since 1950. This pattern held true in 2016, as nearly 98 percent of House incumbents seeking reelection were successful (an additional five lost bids for renomination and are not included in this calculation). What accounts for such high reelection rates? Political scientists have identified several possible factors.[21]

One factor thought to contribute to high reelection rates are the largely homogeneous districts in which many House members run. House districts must be redrawn every ten years to reflect shifts in population across states and within them. In many instances, district lines are drawn to enhance the electoral prospects of the party responsible for the redistricting process by packing opposition party voters into a relatively small number of districts to dilute their influence in the remaining districts.[22] This process, commonly known as "gerrymandering," can place more emphasis on primary elections in heavily partisan districts where the general election outcome is a foregone conclusion.

In 2016, some House members in three states had to run in newly drawn districts because of court challenges to the redistricting plans enacted by their states following the 2010 census. In North Carolina and Virginia, federal courts ruled that the existing districts had been drawn to minimize the influence of African American voters. Florida's congressional districts were found to be in violation of a state law designed to prohibit partisan gerrymanders. The new districts had an important impact on the 2016 election results. Three of the five incumbents who lost primaries were in these states; in North Carolina, the 2nd district primary forced two incumbents to compete for the same seat. Of the 13 seats that flipped from one party to the other in the general election, six were in Florida and Virginia. Moreover, nine of the 33 House members who chose not to run for reelection were from these three states, although redistricting may not have been a factor for all of them.

A second advantage held by incumbent legislators is their access to money to fund their campaigns. On average, House incumbents raised $1.5 million to support their reelection campaigns in 2016, while the average challenger raised only $214,465. Candidates for open seats raised nearly $600,000 on average.[23] Political Action Committees (PACs) gave overwhelmingly to incumbents, with most giving only small amounts to challengers and open seat candidates.[24] These figures mask several important facts about the role of money in congressional elections. First, there is substantial variation in the amount of money raised by candidates in each category. For example, House Speaker Paul Ryan, a Wisconsin Republican, raised almost $19 million in the 2015–2016 election cycle. David Trone, a businessman running for an open seat in Maryland, lost his bid for the Democratic nomination despite spending more than $13 million of his own money. Most candidates spend considerably less. Second, challengers who are successful are typically well funded. In 2016, the average winning challenger spent almost $2 million compared to about $2.5 million spent by the incumbents they defeated. In races where in the incumbents won, they outspent their challengers by a 7-to-1 ratio ($1.2 million to $171,000). Spending was more balanced in open seat contests, with winners outspending their opponents $1.3 million to $737,000.[25] Put simply, money (or the lack of it) still matters. Finally, much of the spending in congressional elections is outside the control of the candidates themselves. PACs and other groups are able to spend money to influence election outcomes so long as their efforts remain independent of the candidates they support. In the open seat race for Nevada's 3rd congressional district, the major party candidates spent a combined $2.5 million on their race. Outside groups spent more than five times that much to influence the election.

A third important advantage held by incumbents is their name recognition. One reason challengers need campaign resources is to introduce themselves to prospective voters. Incumbents generally start with higher levels of name recognition, in part because they have campaigned successfully for election in the past. In a year when much attention was focused on the presidential race, the obstacles to lesser-known challengers' getting their messages out may have been especially daunting.

Donald Trump campaigned for the presidency with a message of change after eight years of Barack Obama. He promised to "drain the swamp" of Washington if he was elected. Ironically, many voters opted to "drain the swamp" by sending the same people back to represent them in Congress.

Diversity in Congress

Although change is slow, the U.S. Congress increasingly looks like the rest of the country. Twenty-one women will serve in the Senate, up one from the previous high of 20 in the previous congress. All four of the newly elected women are Democrats. In addition, two female incumbents were reelected (Republican Lisa Murkowski of Alaska and Democrat Patty Murray of Washington). Three of the four newly elected female senators are women of color.[26] Although ten women were elected to the House as part of the incoming class of new legislators, the total number of women serving will decline from 84 to 83. Thirty-four are women of color; all but three of those women are Democrats.

Travis Long/Raleigh News & Observer/TNS via Getty Images

North Carolina's incumbent governor, Pat McCrory, addresses supporters on election night alongside his wife, Ann. McCrory conceded to his opponent, state Attorney General Roy Cooper, on December 5, 2016, after a partial recount failed to eliminate Cooper's 10,000 vote advantage.

The number of openly LGBT members of Congress remains unchanged. Tammy Baldwin of Wisconsin is the only LGBT member of the Senate. Baldwin and all six LGBT House members are Democrats.

The new congress will be more racially diverse, too, with record numbers of Asian American (12 in the House and 3 in the Senate), Hispanic American (34 in the House and 4 in the Senate), and African American (46 in the House and 3 in the Senate) lawmakers.[27]

Nearly all members of Congress identify as Christian, but the number of non-Christians will increase slightly following the 2016 elections. The number of Jewish members of Congress will increase from 28 to 30. Three newly elected Hindus will bring the total for that faith tradition to four. The number of Muslim and Buddhist legislators remains at two and three, respectively.[28]

The 2016 Elections in the States

In addition to the national offices discussed so far, thousands of candidates campaigned for state and local offices during the 2016 election cycle. State legislatures often provide a gateway to higher office; roughly half of all members of Congress previously served in their state legislatures. In addition, voters in some states had the opportunity to vote directly on questions of public policy. In a federal system, where state and national governments operate separate spheres of policy, these elections are important in their own right.

Governors and State Legislatures

Twelve states held elections for governor in 2016. In five of those states, the candidate who won the governorship came from the party that did not win the state's Electoral College votes. Gubernatorial elections can be influenced by national tides, but issues on the minds of voters are often closer to home.

The last governorship to be decided was in North Carolina. On election night, incumbent Governor Pat McCrory trailed state Attorney General Roy Cooper by about 10,000 votes out of more than 4.6 million cast. McCrory, a Republican, claimed that he was a victim of massive vote fraud. North Carolina's electoral votes went to Donald Trump, who alleged vote fraud in some states but not North Carolina. Although McCrory's campaign provided little evidence to support his claims, the state Board of Elections authorized a partial recount of approximately 94,000 ballots in Durham County (home of Duke University and North Carolina Central University). The recount yielded little change in the results, and McCrory conceded defeat on December 5.

The dynamics of the Indiana governor's race changed when incumbent Governor Mike Pence was selected to be Trump's vice presidential running mate. Pence was being challenged by Democrat John Gregg, whom he had defeated by a narrow margin in 2012. Pence's prospects for reelection had been damaged after he signed Indiana's Religious Freedom Restoration Act into law in 2015. Opponents of the legislation argued that it targeted LGBT people for discrimination. At the time Trump selected him, Pence held a narrow lead in what looked like it would be another close election. He was replaced in the governor's race by Lieutenant Governor Eric Holcomb. The Trump–Pence ticket carried Indiana by a large margin, and Holcomb benefitted in defeating Gregg, 51%–45%.

According to the National Conference of State Legislatures, 2016 was largely a status quo election year at the state legislative level. Republicans increased their share of more than 7,000 state legislative seats nationwide by about 40, and they control a majority of seats in 66 legislative chambers to the Democrats' 30 (the Connecticut Senate is tied). Only three states have legislatures with different parties controlling each legislative chamber.[29]

Ballot Proposals

Many states allow citizens to vote directly on matters of public policy in elections. Some ballot measures are generated by citizens, and others are put on the ballot by state legislatures. Some critics argue that ballot proposals give voters the sense that they are in control of policy making, but the agenda is being set by moneyed interests at the expense of the general good.[30] In 2016, citizens in 35 states considered 154 ballot measures. Nearly three-fourths of the proposals initiated by citizens were approved, as were 83% of the proposals generated by state legislatures.

Drew Angerer/Getty Images

An activist carries a sign promising "It's Not Over" during a protest against Donald Trump's election in New York's Union Square on November 9. Indeed, the full effects of the elections of 2016 remain to be seen: not only for grassroots organizing on the left, but for the political class, the mass media, and the study of political science.

One of the most popular topics for ballot proposals involved marijuana. Four states approved the medical use of marijuana, and an additional four states voted to decriminalize the recreational use of marijuana by adults. Only one state (Arizona) voted down a pot-related measure this year. In general, proposals dealing with marijuana are generated by citizens rather than legislatures.

Another popular topic in 2016 was the minimum wage. Four states (Arizona, Colorado, Maine, and Washington) voted to raise the minimum wage for workers in their states. Minimum wage legislation is often difficult to pass through the traditional legislative process.

Putting the 2016 Election into Context

For many longtime observers of politics, the 2016 presidential election was unlike anything they had experienced. Millions of citizens—including some who usually pay scant attention to politics—ricocheted between feelings of anger, disgust, disappointment, elation, embarrassment, and pride as the campaign unfolded. Donald Trump's ascendency to the White House surprised experts and nonexperts alike.

For political scientists, this election cycle will deepen our understanding of politics and elections by forcing a reexamination of the theories used to explain how the political world works. Some theories will need to be discarded completely, but others will survive with minor tweaks based on new information generated by the Trump and Clinton campaigns.

At the same time, much of what we know about elections remains intact. We could have predicted four years ago that the 2016 election would be close, and it was. We could have predicted that voters would want change after eight years of the Democrats controlling the White House, and that most incumbent members of Congress would be reelected. The campaign offered entertaining twists and turns, but the election ultimately returned to its fundamentals.

As we begin the peaceful transition of power from President Obama to President-elect Trump, many questions about the Trump presidency remain unanswered. Most presidents come to office having articulated a clear vision for public policy over the course of the campaign, and they use the start of their terms in office to push that agenda through Congress. Trump was reluctant to dive into the nuts and bolts of public policy during the campaign, instead falling back on slogans ("Make America Great Again") without saying how the lofty goals were to be accomplished. Will Republicans in Congress take the lead on policy making in a Trump administration? If so, which Republican faction will prevail? Will Trump's cabinet, which is just now taking shape (and is subject to Senate approval), be given the authority to craft policy proposals on behalf of the Administration? Or will President Trump take control of the policy agenda and dictate its passage through Congress and the executive branch bureaucracy? These questions remain unanswered, but political scientists and others will be watching to see what happens.

Trump is taking office as an extremely unpopular president. Will he be able to unite the American people as his predecessors have tried—and mostly failed—to do? What impact will his low popularity have on the passage of his policy agenda?

Perhaps most importantly, candidate Trump campaigned as a populist, advocating protectionist trade policies and a hard line against immigration and dissent. Will President Trump follow the same path? Or will he govern in a manner favoring Wall Street rather than Main Street, the wealthy and powerful rather than the working class, the establishment that tried to undermine his campaign rather than the voters who propelled him to victory?

And what of the Democrats? Will they feel like they need to reinvent the party that won the popular vote for president in 2016 (and in five of the six elections that preceded it)? Will they work with President Trump or obstruct his agenda to make him a one-term president?

For now, one can only speculate—and prepare to watch as history unfolds.

Notes

1. Gary C. Jacobson. 2015. "How Do Campaigns Matter?" *Annual Review of Political Science* 18: 31–47.
2. For a summary of models using fundamental variables to forecast the 2016 election outcome, see James E. Campbell. 2016. "Introduction." *PS: Political Science & Politics* 49(4): 649–654.
3. Source: http://www.pewresearch.org/data-trend/national-conditions/personal-finances/
4. For a summary of models using fundamental variables to forecast the 2016 election outcome, see James E. Campbell. 2016. "Introduction." *PS: Political Science & Politics* 49(4): 649–654.
5. Marty Cohen, David Karol, Hans Noel, and John Zaller. *The Party Decides: Presidential Nominations before and after Reform* (University of Chicago Press, 2009).
6. John H. Aldrich. 1980. "A Dynamic Model of Presidential Nomination Campaigns." *American Political Science Review* 74(3): 651–669.
7. For a list of controversial Trump quotes, see: http://www.ibtimes.com/28-controversial-quotes-future-president-donald-trump-what-next-united-states-2444275
8. Tali Mendelberg. *The Race Card: Campaign Strategy, Implicit Messages, and the Norm of Equality* (Princeton University Press, 2001).
9. Data on fundraising comes from http://www.bloomberg.com/politics/graphics/2016-presidential-campaign-fundraising/ and data on field offices comes from http://fivethirtyeight.com/features/trump-clinton-field-offices/
10. John Sides. September/October 2012. "Do Presidential Debates Really Matter?" *Washington Monthly*.
11. Alan I. Abramowitz and Kyle L. Saunders. 2008. "Is Polarization a Myth?" *The Journal of Politics* 70(2): 542–555.
12. See, for example, Charles S. Taber and Milton Lodge. 2006. "Motivated Skepticism in the Evaluation of Political Beliefs." *American Journal of Political Science* 50(3): 755–769.
13. See Brian F. Schaffner and Cameron J. Roche. 2017. "Misinformation and Motivated Reasoning: Responses to Economic News in a Politicized Environment." *Public Opinion Quarterly*.

14. Thomas M. Holbrook and Scott D. McClurg. 2005. "The Mobilization of Core Supporters: Campaigns, Turnout, and Electoral Composition in United States Presidential Elections." *American Journal of Political Science* 49(4): 689–703.

15. Source: http://fivethirtyeight.com/features/education-not-income-predicted-who-would-vote-for-trump/

16. An example of the economic insecurity narrative can be found here: http://www.cnn.com/2016/11/10/opinions/how-clinton-lost-the-working-class-coontz/. An example of the racism narrative can be found here: http://www.salon.com/2016/11/13/yep-race-really-did-trump-economics-a-data-dive-on-his-supporters-reveals-deep-racial-animosity/. And an example of the sexism narrative can be found here: http://www.usatoday.com/story/opinion/voices/2016/11/10/trump-election-white-women-sexism-racism/93611984/

17. The racism scale was based on the extent to which respondents agreed or disagreed with the following statements: (1) I am angry that racism exists; (2) White people in the U.S. have certain advantages because of the color of their skin; and (3) Racial problems in the U.S. are rare, isolated situations. The sexism scale was based on agreement or disagreement with the following statements: (1) Many women are actually seeking special favors, such as hiring policies that favor them over men, under the guise of asking for "equality"; (2) Women are too easily offended; (3) Women seek to gain power by getting control over men; and (4) When women lose to men in a fair competition, they typically complain about being discriminated against.

18. Michael Tessler. November 22, 2016. "Views about Race Mattered More in Electing Trump Than in Electing Obama." *Washington Post*, https://www.washingtonpost.com/news/monkey-cage/wp/2016/11/22/peoples-views-about-race-mattered-more-in-electing-trump-than-in-electing-obama/

19. Harry Enten. November 10, 2016. "There Were No Purple States on Tuesday," http://fivethirtyeight.com/features/there-were-no-purple-states-on-tuesday/

20. Two seats in Louisiana are awaiting runoff elections as of this writing. Both are expected to remain in Republican hands.

21. See, for example, Robert S. Erikson and Gerald E. Wright. "Voters, Candidates, and Issues in Congressional Elections," in *Congress Reconsidered*, 10 ed., edited by Lawrence C. Dodd and Bruce I. Oppenheimer (Thousand Oaks, CA: CQ Press, 2013), 99–103.

22. Bruce I. Oppenheimer. "Deep Red and Blue Congressional Districts: The Causes and Consequences of Declining Party Competitiveness," in *Congress Reconsidered*, 8th ed., edited by Lawrence C. Dodd and Bruce I. Oppenheimer (Washington, DC: CQ Press, 2005).

23. The average for challengers and open seats includes some candidates who lost in their primaries. Source: https://www.opensecrets.org/overview/incumbs.php

24. Source: https://www.opensecrets.org/overview/pac2cands.php?cycle=2016

25. Source: https://www.opensecrets.org/overview/incad.php

26. Kamala Harris of California is of Jamaican and Indian descent, Catherine Cortez-Masto of Nevada is Latina, and the mother of Tammy Duckworth of Illinois is from Thailand. See Christina Marcos. November 17, 2016. "115th Congress Will Be Most Racially Diverse in History." *The Hill*, http://thehill.com/homenews/house/306480-115th-congress-will-be-most-racially-diverse-in-history.

27. Marcos, "115th Congress Will Be Most Racially Diverse in History."

28. Marcos, "115th Congress Will Be Most Racially Diverse in History."

29. Tim Storey. December 2016. "Moving Ahead." *State Legislatures*, 10–13.

30. David S. Broder. *Democracy Derailed: Initiative Campaigns and the Power of Money* (New York: Harcourt, 2000).

About the Authors

Brian Schaffner is a Professor in the Department of Political Science at the University of Massachusetts Amherst and a faculty associate at the Institute for Quantitative Social Science at Harvard University. He is also the Founding Director of the UMass Poll and a co-PI for the Cooperative Congressional Election Study. Schaffner's research focuses on public opinion, campaigns and elections, political parties, and legislative politics. He is the coauthor of the book *Campaign Finance and Political Polarization: When Purists Prevail,* the coeditor of the book *Winning with Words: The Origins & Impact of Political Framing*, and coauthor of *Understanding Political Science Research Methods: The Challenge of Inference.* His research has also appeared in over thirty journal articles.

John A. Clark is a Professor and Chair of the Department of Political Science at Western Michigan University. Clark's research focuses on political parties, campaigns and elections, legislative politics, and the politics of the American South. He is the coeditor of *Southern Political Party Activists* and *Party Organization and Activism in the American South*, which won the 1999 V. O. Key Award as the best book on Southern politics. He has authored or coauthored more than thirty book chapters and articles in scholarly journals. Since 2002, he and Schaffner have coauthored a series of short monographs analyzing the presidential and midterm elections; 2016 marks the eighth in the series.